Spirit Within, Spirits Throughout

"If courage is a tangible, durable, and renewable resource, it comes directly from the sources of spirit that Tiyi Schippers identifies in these poems—the living world dancing around us, the ancestors and all whom we love, our own deep wellspring of soul and awareness. She has thought deeply about *how hearts born of thunder/grow stronger and harder/even torn asunder* and urges us to celebrate fleeting but abundant manifestations of spirit—*a bird flashing by the window/the flick of a squirrel's tail/brief, bright sun amid thick clouds/the sound of the back door/ ... /in the seconds before/love enters the room.* Grief for her is *a living thing* but she has learned *from it/we rise/in poetry/in song/in art.* This is a book you will want to keep by your side, one that invites the reader to welcome *the sacred ... into spark.*"

—**Ruelaine Stokes,** poet & spoken word artist, author of *Jar of Plenty*

Spirit Within,Spirits Throughout

A Spiritual Exploration Through Poetry

Antoinette "Tiyi" Schippers

Parkhurst Brothers Publishers
MARION, MICHIGAN

www.parkhurstbrothers.com

Consumers may order Parkhurst Brothers books from their favorite online or bricks-and-mortar booksellers, expecting prompt delivery. Parkhurst Brothers books are distributed to the trade through the Chicago Distribution Center. Trade and library orders may be placed through Ingram Book Company, Baker & Taylor, Follett Library Resources and other book industry wholesalers. To order from Chicago Distribution Center, phone 1-800-621-2736 or fax to 800-621-8476. Copies of this and other Parkhurst Brothers Publishers titles are available to organizations and corporations for purchase in quantity by contacting Special Sales Department at our home office location, listed on our web site. Manuscript submission guidelines for this publishing company are available at our web site.

Printed in the United States of America
First Edition, September 2022
Printing history: 2022 2022 2023   8 7 6 5 4 3 2 1

Library Cataloging Data
1.   Author—Antoinette Schippers, American teacher, musician, poet, and author
2.   Subject—Poetry, Americana
3.   Subject—Spirituality
4.   Subject—Spirit
2022-trade paperback and e-book

ISBN: Trade Paperback   978-1-62491-189-7
ISBN: e-book   978-1-62491-190-3

Cover Image Credit: Photo 1862685 | ©Werner Wilmes | Dreamstime.com

Parkhurst Brothers Publishers believes the free and open exchange of ideas is essential for the maintenance of our freedoms. We support the First Amendment of the United States Constitution and encourage all citizens to study all sides of public policy questions, and to make up their own minds.

Cover and interior design by   Linda D. Parkhurst PhD
Acquired for Parkhurst Brothers Publishers by   Ted Parkhurst

092022

I dedicate this book to my mother,

Jacquelin Liautaud Schippers (1931-2018),

a writer of beautiful things, and the one who taught me to listen to spirit, and to trust my heart as well as my mind.

Acknowledgements

I wish to thank friends and family who have responded to my poetry and encouraged me to continue to write. I also want to acknowledge those who raised me in a way that allowed me to take the time to notice the world as it passes, and inspired me to express my feelings and observations through art.

Contents

GRIEF

1

Grief
is a blood red rose
that pierces my skin
with sharp persistent thorns
as once fragrant petals
wither and fall,
leaving me bleeding,
gripping ever more tightly to
grief.

2

I saw an old friend today
after a long
and arduous
year.
I held a dear friend today
after a distant
and strenuous
year.
I wept with a loved friend today
after a lonely
and onerous
year.

3
평화 (Peace)

I wonder when we will learn peace, or even if we ever will.
Like wishing the clouds would disperse allowing warm sun to
shine through
as thunder roars over hillsides and cold hard rain soaks me to
the bone.

4

Waking from a dream
I think I should call my mom
then I remember.

5

Sometimes I ponder
how hearts born of thunder
grow stronger and harder
even torn asunder.

6

Two years
since
my mother
transitioned
from body to
light,
from pain to
peace,
from here to
everywhere.

7

Here
in this quiet place of remembering
I know gratitude.
Here
in this tranquil place of remembering
I know connection.
Here
in this powerful place of remembering
I know love.

8
RBG

Light a candle tonight.
Hold it high
against the darkness.
A great warrior has passed.
A defender of justice,
defender of democracy.
A brilliant mind that held
a brilliant flame.
Our nation is darker tonight,
but the universe glows
with her brilliance.
Rise up!
Rise up
and kindle that spark!
Kindle that flame
in your own soul!
Let us mourn,
then let us rise
to carry that spark
onward.

9
Brother

Today I will pause to remember.
Today I'll be still and reflect.
A full year without you beside us,
filled with bittersweet retrospect.
Today I'll remember your laughter,
allowing your love to console.
Knowing that here ever after,
my brother lives on in my soul.

10
Isolation

Goldfish in the tank
push against glass enclosure.
Now we understand.

11

It has been one year
since this man's impactful life
synthesized to tale.

12

What I am learning about grief
is that it is a seed.
A seed from which can grow a bramble,
or a rose,
a willow,
or an oak.

A seed that cracks open, raw and tender,
splitting itself apart,
as tiny shoots push toward the light.

What I am learning about grief,
is that it is a living thing,
housed in a shell,
until rain,
tears,
make it swell to bursting,
burst to living,
live to being.

What I am learning about grief,
is that from it,
we rise,
in poetry,
in song,
in art.
Together or apart,
reaching for the light.

13

We gathered on a hillside
that overlooks the sea.
Beneath the branches springing,
as early birds were singing
a quiet place to abide
through eternity.
We gathered on a hillside
that overlooks the sea.

We gathered in the springtime
though it was barely green.
With early blossoms shining,
the widow's heart was pining,
reflecting on a lifetime
that had so fleeting been.
We gathered in the springtime
though it was barely green.

We gathered there in mourning
To celebrate his life.
We left the hillside ringing
with many voices singing,
a musical adorning
of rock, and sea, and sky.
We gathered there in mourning
to celebrate his life.

We gathered under red pines
beside the ancient stones.
We huddled close together
against the chilly weather,
where pain and love entwined,
both now and long ago.
We gathered under red pines
beside the ancient stones.

We gathered, though unwilling,
beside a new dug grave.
From near and distant places,
love, differences erases.
All eyes with tears were filling,
though trying to be brave.
We gathered, though unwilling,
beside a new dug grave.

We gathered for our loved one,
a kind and gentle soul.
Who loved his wife and daughter.
Who treasured Great Lakes water.
Who's dance with death had begun
before he would grow old.
We gathered for our loved one,
a kind and gentle soul.

14

Equinox has passed
and my altar remains dark.
Mourning's not broken.

15

With too much in mind
I slip beneath cool linens
and turn out the light.

16

I would say

I miss you my mama,

but...

It would deny your constant presence

in my heart,

my mind,

my soul.

17

It's almost midnight
and still my mind keeps spinning
to keep me from sleep.

18

On this day that honors mothers,
I traveled to a place of remembering.
Stepping onto the soft earth
I felt unspeakable grief,
as I walked among the ancient graves
of children lost.
I felt mothers'
powerless,
panicked,
perdition
that claimed their
own.
I respect,
and remember
each of your
broken hearts.

19

That which breaks us,
leaves hearts
shattered
in piles of rubble,
raining down
on our
weary souls
leaving us
fragile,
frayed,
ferocious.

20

Sometimes,
as the sun falls
below the horizon,
I feel grief rise.
I sense the coming
darkness,
and loneliness sets in.
So much has changed.
So much lost.
So much
passes far too quickly.
I feel ancient,
weary,
waning,
like the daylight.
Then...
my grandchild
bursts in
smiling
to tell me of her play.
To demonstrate
how she learned
hopscotch,
and for a hug.

HOPE

1
Awakening

First warm rain
splashes outside my window
stepping on crabapple branches.
Dancing above my head
with tiny steady footfalls on the roof.
Thunder rolls over the hill
and the dance becomes
fevered
frenzied
wild.
The air cools with the pungent scent
of Earth
awakening
as I prepare for
my own
awakening
in dreams.

2
The First of May

On top of the ridge on the first of May,
I gaze at the river below.
The spring lies out of my reach today,
but her graces I still can behold.

I make an offering to the ones
who guard this sacred place:
an amber stone that catches sun,
for water, and vision, and grace.

Wind groans over the tops of the trees,
as they gracefully bend and sway.
I watch in the wood among early spring green,
all on the first of May.

3

Here,
Now,
spring rain
falling hard
against my window
scenting the air for sweetest dreams.

4

Baby steps!
As we do this hard work,
facing frailty,
facing history,
facing reality.

Giant steps!
As we do this heart work,
changing reality,
changing deficiency,
changing bigotry.

Rising steps!
As we do this hard, heart work,
raising unity,
raising liberty,
raising accountability.

5

In the long year apart I learned
connection does not require
proximity.
Kindness is stronger than
fear.
Love can transcend
darkness.
Knowledge grew more
Precious,
truth more
fragile.
In troubled times we learned
who we
are,
what we
are,
what we can
endure,
and how we must rise
together,
even
when
apart.

6

Tiny buds emerge
as epitome of hope
on undressed branches.

7

First we came from the water,
second we rose from the mire.
Third we fell from the ether,
and fourth we grew from the fire.

Fifth we gathered together.
Sixth, we formed separate clans.
Seventh we ousted the other,
eighth we all took our stands.

Ninth we marched off to battle,
tenth we found new ways to kill.
Eleventh we brought the death rattle,
twelfth we conquered the hill.

Thirteenth we surveyed the carnage,
fourteenth we surveyed our souls.
Fifteenth we faced our own damage,
sixteenth we longed to be whole.

Seventeenth we looked to each other,
eighteenth we reached out our hands.
Nineteenth we saw sisters and brothers,
as one sacred spirit at last.

8
Springtime

Springtime is a crocus,
poking through April snow,
reaching for a warming sun.
Imminent,
never timid.
Growing in harshness.
Tenacious,
ineffable,
making her surprising
entrance.
Springtime!

9
Winter Solstice

I am not afraid of the darkness.
I am not afraid of the icy winds that blow.
I am not afraid of the storm,
or wind,
or snow.
I know,
it will all be right.
As long as we stand,
hand in hand,
on this the longest night.

10

For every moment,
even for the tears that fall,
I am still grateful.

11

After the storm
summer
drifts in the open window.
As scent of
blossoms, earth, and green
dance on my skin,
mingling in my senses
and soul.
Calling
spirit to join the wicking,
to join in the spiral
of life
borne anew

12

April arrived in the night
oblivious of troubles.
Blind to fear.
Heedless of the cry
to isolate.
April slipped in
on a chilly breeze
shrouded in gray,
hidden in the promise of spring.

13

Cold hard rain falls now
outside my open window.
Still I feel the moon.

14

May Grandmother Moon
remind us
that light exists,
even in darkness.

May Grandmother Moon
remind us
that we must be that light,
even in darkness.

15

In the darkness now
as wind throws its weight around.
I sure can relate.

16

Sun has fallen,
pale indigo in the west.
Moonlight teases the eastern sky,
before she rises above the trees.
So much gives us hope
within hints of light,
before rising
above the trees.
Remember to
remember,
as the world shifts,
and only hints of light appear
to guide us
forward.
Remember.

17
Observation On Isolation

One can only see the magnificent form of a snowflake
when it is alone,
apart from the rest.
Among others it is a drift, a blanket, a dusting, a covering.
Alone it is a brilliant star,
bright and lovely.

18

At the Niibeshone
singing a song of healing
for the Earth's people.

19

Finding my bed after these most difficult days
I give thanks for dear,
dear friends.
For love
learned over many years.
For truth telling
without waiting for the right time,
and for music…
Music that binds us,
and music that breaks our hearts,
then fills the gaping crevice with sound,
lovingly made
together.
Life and love are so precious,
and so precarious.
Waste not a single moment to
throw your head back.
Let salt tears blend with harmony,
creating
catharsis in song.

20

The air grows still.
Looking through my window
I imagine myself
among the blooms
of the crabapple.
Humming with bees,
opening with blossoms,
unfurling with young leaves.
I embody the fullness of her,
awakening,
Spreading her branches
full of delicate pink wonders,
that survived the afternoon wind
that shook so many loose.
I too hold on
despite wind,
or torrent,
or trial.

We,
the crabapple and I,
bloom
boldly,
audacious,
unafraid,
in these brief
splendid
moments.

LOVE

1

Good friends,
like early warm breezes.
Like the sweet, faint scent
of untouched blossoms.

Sweet friends,
like air smelling of earth.
Like the aroma of hope
and summer's promise.

Old friends,
like crisp autumn days.
Like vibrant leaves radiant
in the last warm sun.

True friends,
like warm fire lit evenings.
Like glowing red embers
against winter's chill

2
Sister

Sharing a life story.
History.
Herstory.
Sharing the same branches
enhances
our chances
of sharing our hearts.
Not apart,
but a part

3
Crabapple

Waiting for Sol's warm kiss to coax them forth
delicate buds cling tightly
to a crabapple branch.

Waiting for love's warm kiss to coax them forth
tentative hearts cling tightly
to a scant outside chance.

4

When the weather turned colder
snowflakes swirled
in an April sky.
Porch plants found respite,
cozily gathered
by the hearth.
Tender blossoms appeared
confused,
shivering in their newly
made beds.
Still, I leave the window
above my own bed
wide open,
Inhaling the chilly night air,
I tuck warmly
beneath layers
of down.
Dreaming,
dreaming,
dreaming
of a time
when the weather turned warmer.

5

Stillness falls
as they drive
away.
Car filled
to the brim
with family,
and love.

Still, in these walls
as the echoes
fade,
heart filled
to the brim
with memories
and love.

6

Remembering
my mother's green eyes.
Her boisterous laugh.
Her warmest embraces.
The lines of her hand.
My mother's wise counsel.
Her enormous heart
that fills every moment,
or crevice,
or distance,
with love.

7
Ode To The Desert Sun

Ah bright,
relentless lover!
Breathing light and heat.
You laugh as I take cover,
beneath awnings in the street.

As I seek shadows by the walls,
you laughingly remind,
how in my frigid northern halls,
I'd move my body nigh.

How I savored every shard,
that slipped through frozen air,
and how I sought your warm regard,
that kindled our affair.

Now in your driest bower,
I am shrinking from your light.
Not due to lover's power,
but your power to,
ignite.

8

From a safe distance
I look in your loving eyes
longing for your touch.

9

Connection, I learned,
does not need proximity,
only awareness.

10

Old friends,
like skin
that holds us in.
Longtime friends like wind
that blows us in.
Sweet friends
like kin
that flows within.
Dear friends
leave love
where they have been.

11
Gratitude

Staring into the abyss,
empty,
lost,
and alone.
Enveloped in darkness
I whisper
Thank you.

12

I noticed the Calla Lily drooping,
clustered among other plants
under the window.
Her leaves lying limp
against her pot.

"Have you watered the plants?"
I called to him across the house.
"Oh dear," he said
whisking her away to the kitchen
for a drink of fresh water
to nurture
and replenish.

I noticed the man I love reading.
Sitting among thriving plants
under the window,
His woolen cap perched
against the chill.

Have I watered the plants?
I ask myself across the room.
"I love you." I say.
He smiles warmly at me as I write.
"I love you too," he tells me.
We nurture
and replenish.

13
Thanksgiving

I feel my mother
leaning in over pots
smiling on my work.

14

Old friends, like embers in the fire
warming the chill on winter nights,
lifting our spirits from the mire,
sparking memories of delights
when we were all mere acolytes.
Seeking wonders along the way.
Pushing the limits to new heights.
Bringing us wisdom for this day

15

For all the good men I have loved:
The men who sang children to sleep.
Men who carried them on their backs... or shoulders.
The men who taught their sons to be gentle,
and their daughters to be strong in a world that expects the
opposite.
Men with ready, open hearts and easy tears.
The men who know when to listen, letting others lead.
The men who alone, or side by side with the partners they
love, carry generations into the future.
I love and honor you.

16

As twilight fades
muting vibrant spring greens
I fall on to cool linens,
letting my body
and spirit
sink into
the freshness of nightfall,
following a day awash
in mists
and bursts
of color.

17
Full Flower Blood Moon

Grandmother hid her face
behind thick clouds.
It's been months
since I've seen her
with my eyes.
What should be radiant,
remained reclusive.
What could inspire
remained illusive.
and yet,
a new poem.

18
Moonlit Dreaming

Moon reaches in
kissing my skin.

Stars overhead
shine on this bed.

Delicate beams
bring me sweet dreams.

19

Sitting alone in this candlelight,
watching shadows dance before me
as the flame flits and flickers
with each breath that I take
poetry comes forth
from a sacred
font within
deepest
soul.

20

I have seen you in the morning,
In the sunlight through the window,
On the pillow, on the bed, where we have lain.

I have known only you in my deepest heart.

Though there were others when we were younger,
When we were wilder, when we were stronger.
We held them close for a while then fell away.

I have touched only you in my deepest heart.

Now we are older. What does it matter?
A little wiser, a little sadder.
I only know one thing for sure that I can say.

I have loved only you in my deepest heart.

And I have seen you in the midnight,
In the moonlight through the window,
On the pillow, on the bed, where we have lain.

I have known only you in my deepest heart.

SPIRIT

1

On the eve of Beltane,
my spirit seeks embers,
in fire, and forest,
and green.

On the eve of Beltane,
the old world engenders.
The pyre and promise,
unseen.

On the eve of Beltane,
my old soul remembers.
Inspired, I'm querist
and queen.

2

I went to the forest to dream,
where bright faerie spirits I've seen.
And tender blossoms shine,
amid dry leaves and fallen wood.
Observing in silence I stood,
by sacred oak and pine.

3

Remembering how I saw,
somewhere in the distant past,
long before I learned to see,
with wizened eyes, open to light unsurpassed.

4

Awaken that which has been
sleeping.
Arise to what is
new.
Abandon that which has been
poison.
Resign to what is
true.
Acknowledge that which had been
hidden.
Accede to what we
knew.

5

Deep in the dark and the blackness of night,
I escape to a place quite well hidden.
My spirit rises with wonder-filled sight,
as I follow the path where I'm bidden.

Into this strange world I willingly go,
seeking ancestors' marvelous wisdom.
To find what my great, great grandmothers know,
and attempt to encompass their vision.

So into places beyond corporeal,
I relinquish my spirit to wander,
an ephemeral world, also quite real,
leads my mind and my spirit to ponder.

How wonders as these, revealed in the night,
serve to inspire, and further insight.

6

Full Wolf Moon rising,
illuminating a path
that lies before me.

7

Sunrise at The Pine
gathering cold, clear, water
for my ritual.

8

Welcoming the dark
on this long Solstice night.
Calling in the spark
that kindles my small light.

9

Eternity,
spoken in
abstract
terms.

Eternity,
pictured in
distanced
words.

Eternity,
visioned in
entranced
worlds.
Eternity lies
within.

10

Fall

between two skies.

Fall

between air and water.

Fall

between image and imagine.

Fall

Between.

11

On my bed at last.
The open window,
pulls a cool, late summer breeze,
across my skin.
It plays with the candle flame,
that plays with the shadow,
that plays with the light,
that plays with my spirit.
Alone,
yet, not.

On my bed at last.
The open window,
pulls the scent of soft rain,
into my senses.

It plays with the candle flame,
that plays with the shadow,
that plays with the light,
that plays with my spirit,
Alone,
yet, not.

Alone, yet not.

12
Grandmother Moon

Grandmother Moon swells to fullness.
We welcome her.
Illuminating vastness
of darkness,
of spiritlessness,
of soullessness.

Grandmother Moon bares her soul
as Sol retreats
beneath horizons,
out of sight,
out of light
into night,
into rite.

Grandmother Moon beckons her people,
and we welcome the sacred,
out of dark,
out of heart,
into arc,
into spark.

13
Beltane

Just before the morning dawn
on this, the first of May.
The birds began their early song,
and bid me to awake.

I rose all in the cool of spring
to greet this blessed day.
With all my soul remembering
a world lifetimes away.

So to the holy well I go
in search of clarity.
Preparing hands, and heart, and soul
to call the sacred SHE.

Lighting five candles and sweet herbs
I gazed beyond the glass,
welcoming CREATOR HER.
May wisdom come to pass.

May light and healing blessed be,
awakening each soul.
Surrender to reality
as ancient truths unfold.

14

At my altar tonight
candles burn low.
I feel
memories
enter
this
space.
At my altar tonight
candles burn low.
I feel
ancestors
enter
this
space.
At my altar tonight
candles burn low.
I feel
loved ones
enter
this
space.

At my altar tonight
candles burn low.
I feel
    eternity
        enter
            this
                space.
At my altar tonight.

15

Heal the great wound.
That which has separated us

each

from the other,
from our souls,
from our senses,
from the Earth,
from the sacred.

Heal the great wound.
That which will connect us

each

into the other,
into our souls,
into our senses,
into the Earth,
into the sacred.

16

Listen to the shadows.
You will hear all you need.
Light is hidden there.

17

I went to the spring
seeking a healing spirit
as gentle rain fell.

18

Smelling of woodsmoke
my crescive heart and spirit
release and arise.

19

Good Spirit
of the Sacred Place
grant me blessing, grant me grace.
Keep me safe in night and day,
and hold me ever in your sway.
Spirit of water, earth, and green,
grant me sight for things unseen.

20

Sitting before these bright candles
my curious spirit rambles
in a world well hidden.
I open my eyes for seeing,
as my spirit rises, heeding,
to fly where I'm bidden.

TRANSCENDENCE

1
In the Predawn Dark

Reflecting on dreams
Recalling details

Examining content
Exploring context

Seeking insight
Smiling inside

2

In the cold night
Candles shone bright

Folks gathered round
Lifting the sound

Singing a song
Making us strong

Let freedom ring
Let us *all* sing

Powerful choice
To raise each voice

3

Wondering,
as my thoughts
wander.
Full of
wonder,
feeling fonder
for wonderful
reminders.
I ponder
wonder!

4

Sometimes
when I listen
within memory,
I hear your voice.
I recall
words you spoke,
and smile,
recalling
your smile,
your eyes,
radiating love

Sometimes
when I listen
within stillness,
I feel your love
deeply.
No longer in memory,
but here, now,
and I know you are
here,
now,
still.

5

I sit before my candles,
on this frozen winter night.
My soul begins to ramble,
in the flicker of the light.

My amulets and potions,
stand purposely in their place.
Protections, prayers, and totems,
hold me firm in their embrace.

Lighting the herbs and incense,
for my journey to begin.
Smoking away all pretense,
I seek wisdom once again.

And so here, at my altar,
my most sacred spirit place,
all trepidation falters,
when enlightenment awaits.

6

I don't talk about pain.
It's not something on which I dwell.
Instead I push it away
and soldier on

Though I am not a soldier,
I don't talk about pain.
It makes me weary,
yet strong somehow.

But some days I don't feel strong.
Some days hurt more than others.
I don't talk about pain.
I just feel it.

But feeling pain hasn't thwarted me,
nor hindered my vision or soul,
nor kept me from joy.
I don't talk about pain.

7

Into a bright and frozen winter sky,
I watch a raven rise, and take to wing.
Her feathers catch the light as she goes by,
and shimmer like my soul awakening.

I watch her as she dances in the air,
above the earth all clothed in winter snow.
I long to find my wings and join her there.
Alas, I only watch her from below.

The raven swoops and perches in a tree,
along with other ravens gathered near.
I see her turn and cast her gaze at me.
The two of us, from different worlds, cohere.

8

Candle flames burned bright on,
this most blessed night.
Faces gathered round them,
shone in softest light.

Friends and loved ones sharing,
in the amber glow.
Whisp'ring heart's desires,
ever long ago.

Though we may not gather,
as in days of yore,
still the flame igniting,
kindles as before.

Calling in our muses,
this cross quarter day.
Re-creation calls and,
holds us in her sway.

Ever we'll remember,
though the world grow cold.
Carrying the wisdom,
ancient ones foretold.

Let the candles flame grow,
brighter in the dark.
Let the light within us,
burst forth from our hearts.

9

Coconut oil
melts
into my
ashy
winter
skin.

My mother used
Vaseline,
or
olive oil,
sometimes even
butter
on her hands.

I inherited her skin,
and her green eyes,
and her love,
and her history,
and her resilience,
and her strength,
and her stories

and
her,
and
her,
and
her.

I feel her
melt
like
coconut oil
into my
ashy
winter
skin.

10

In these troubled times,
when human suffering is so
cruelly amplified
by the illusion of power.
When the future
seems uncertain
and fear creeps in.
Celebrate the small things.
The fleeting moments.
A bird flashing by the window.
The flick of a squirrel's tail.
Brief, bright sun amid thick clouds.
The sound of the back door,
wondering, "who's there?"
in the seconds before
love enters the room.
The inquisitive smile,
just prior to a hug.

And when you do,
when you do,
you become a poet.
For these fleeting moments,
these small things,
make up the metric,
melodic
magic
of us,
filling a troubled world
with
love.

11

True change rarely occurs without pain,
as we pluck beauty from the profane.

Cutting restraints that hold spirits fast.
Releasing that which harms us at last.

Each of these struggles must be endured
in order for growth to be assured.

Each one of us must go through the fire,
and drag our wounded selves from
the mire.

Rising again in a world anew,
focusing on what we know is true.

Leaving the pain and trouble behind.
Allowing our bright spirit to shine.

12

Let music ease your weary soul.
Let beat and melody take hold.
Let your mind easily slip from the fray.

Lean into the bass and the strings.
Lean into the pleasure it brings.
Lean back and let music take you away.

Feel how music lightens your heart.
Feel how it grabs you from the start.
Feel how great music holds you in its sway.

13

birdsong
through the window
open to morning chill
music to my waking heart and
spirit

14

into the abyss
I willingly go
anticipating

15

Spring comes to the north country
flirting with a chilly wind.
Teasing fragile buds
from shivering branches.

An early morning fog lifts,
exposing Lacey green underthings
before the trees fully dress
for summer.

Dew covered meadows
boldly adorn themselves in
yellow dots of dandelion,
yet blush around the edges
with cast off bud casings.

Spring comes to the north country.
Earth and life awaken.
Songbirds joyfully sing
a love song to the trees.

16

I feel the call of wild things,
water pooled in cool clear springs.

Let me bask in nature's fold
breathing wonders yet untold.

Take me where the spirits dwell.
Take me to the sacred well.

Let me feel the breath of spring
as my soul's remembering

rituals from bygone days
stirring hearts in ancient ways.

On this northern Beltane Eve
nature's spell I seek to weave.

17

When things don't turn out as you thought,
and hope springs less than eternal,
hold fast to what good deeds have wrought,
and release all thoughts infernal.
Take stock of your strength internal,
Keep your focus on what is true.
Then just as the woods grow vernal,
you'll feel the awakening too.

18
In Praise Of Harmony

Voices that blend so sweetly
in tones that can stir one's soul
engage each quite completely
embracing us in their fold.

Lyrics that can inspire
connecting hearts all as one.
Thoughts that kindle desire
for memories long since gone.

Music will lift each spirit
holding each firm in its sway,
thrilling us as we hear it
in a most enchanting way.

19

Are you there?
A question I ask
quite often
when alone
as twilight drains from the sky,
and the night birds call.

20

Sometimes love just wins.
Despite barriers.
Despite judgement.
Love transcends trepidation.
Today... love wins.

About the Author

Antoinette M. (Tiyi) Schippers is an artist, writer, storyteller, and spirit medium who lives in northern Michigan. She is both a poet and a novelist whose debut work, *Beyond Brick and Bone,* was nominated for the Michigan Notable Book Award in 2020. Tiyi earned a BA in Elementary Education with a minor in English language arts from Michigan State University, then taught for forty years. She is a well known Michigan songwriter whose songs have been performed and recorded by numerous artists.

Tiyi comes from a family culture rich in spirit. Her mother's family was part of The Great Migration, escaping the Jim Crow south in New Orleans, to "passe blanc" north to Chicago, bringing with them memories of Hoodoo and Creole rootwork. Her father's family culture was steeped in Irish lore with an open acknowledgment of things that lie beyond corporeal reality. This combination made it not only possible, but inevitable for Tiyi to experience, acknowledge, and nurture her ability to connect with spirit.

Tiyi and her husband delight in four grown children and five grandchildren. She is active in her community serving on several boards as well as serving as Mayor Pro Tem in the city of Cadillac.

If you have enjoyed this book, we recommend you
point your browser to:

www.parkhurstbrothers.com